A
WENTWORTH FOLKINS PORTFOLIO

# THE·GREAT·DAYS·OF CANADIAN STEAM

*Wentworth Folkins* (signature)

TEXT BY WENTWORTH FOLKINS & MICHAEL BRADLEY

The Great Days of Canadian Steam

Copyright © 1988 by Wentworth Folkins

All Rights Reserved

ISBN 0-88882-101-8

*Publisher:*
Anthony Hawke

*Text:*
Wentworth Folkins & Michael Bradley

*Designer:*
Gerard Williams

*Composition:*
Accurate Typesetting Limited

*Third Printing, 1991*

Hounslow Press
A Division of
Anthony R. Hawke Limited
124 Parkview Avenue
Willowdale, Ontario, Canada
M2N 3Y5

Printed and bound in Hong Kong

## CONTENTS

The Making of a Railway Artist / 4

Text & Colour Plates / 8-107

Glossary of Railroad Terms / 108

Index of Colour Plates / 112

To my wife Joan
and to the memory of my father

# THE MAKING OF A RAILWAY ARTIST

Otty Folkins, Wentworth's father, "oiling up" at Cochrane, Ontario, December 1951.

Canadian artist, Wentworth D. Folkins is internationally recognized as one of the world's most accomplished painters of steam railroading subjects. His love of steam trains, and his unusual talent in depicting them, come from close association with railways beginning in childhood. Folkins' father was a railroad man in the early years of this century, the "Golden Age" of steam, and the future artist learned about his complex subject under the guidance of a sympathetic expert. That explains the technical accuracy of Folkins' work, the meticulous attention to detail that has captivated train buffs and collectors of railroad art.

But perhaps the most important aspect of Folkins' work has nothing to do with rendering the mechanics of steam propulsion with exacting accuracy. Folkins does not simply paint trains. *He paints the relevance of trains.* He is an historian who has chronicled an important era of our technological progress with brush and canvas instead of words. His paintings capture what steam transportation *meant* to individuals and society more evocatively than words could express. The many train trips that young Wentworth made with his engineer father during the 1930s and 1940s left an indelible impression of the impact of the railroad on a young and growing country. So, in Folkins' art it is not the trains themselves that will entrance anyone but case-hardened railroad fanatics, but his vignettes of bygone Canadian life that will charm almost everyone. We look at his work and we see ourselves the way we were. But ...

Charm is not a word that is vital enough to describe what happens when you take the time to look at a Folkins painting, when you actually "study" it. The longer you take in one of Folkins' pictures, the stronger the emotional reaction that takes place. Mere pleasure at the remembrance of fond things past is transformed into lump-in-the-throat nostalgia. His trains, you will discover are really time machines that serve to give a focus to a way of life that was simple, secure and more honestly human. Folkins' trains and the jobs they're doing and the people they're serving represent a world far removed from the late 20th century, for better or for worse, a world that was easier to understand and easier to cope with. Perhaps, a world that was more fulfilling in spite of the progress we have made and enjoyed since.

Looking at a painting like "Charlie's World," "Home For Christmas" or "Country Crossing" it is impossible not to suspect that Folkins knows very well that his art is about a vanished people and a vanished lifestyle, not just about steam trains that were supplanted by diesels in the mid-1950s. In fact, one gets the impression that Folkins paints his trains with such painstaking accuracy as a personal defence against allowing nostalgia for a vanished and valuable life-perspective to take over the whole canvas. His trains are hardware, complicated hardware, and they seem to be an intricately created talisman to ward off the artist's, and our own, wistfulness for an epoch lost forever.

Born in Cochrane, Ontario on August 12, 1928, Wentworth Folkins lived in the small northern Ontario community until the 1950s, attending both Primary and High School in the town. Both his father and mother were Maritimers from Saint John and Woodstock, New Brunswick respectively. Because the elder Folkins was a railroad man, the family had a Canadian National pass to travel yearly any-

The Folkins' home in Cochrane, Ontario.

where in North America. But perhaps it is significant that most of the early trips that Wentworth Folkins remembers were back to the Maritimes, especially New Brunswick. Later, with his engineer father, Wentworth travelled in CN locomotive cabs to places like Senneterre and Tachereau in Quebec, Hearst and Nakina in Ontario. Aboard CN ships, he travelled to the Saguenay, Sarnia and Duluth.

For a family that had a rail pass for a yearly trip "anywhere in North America" these places do not represent prime tourist destinations. Quite obviously, the Folkins family were small-town people. They lived in a small town, chose to visit small towns. They understood small towns.

This is not to say that young Wentworth Folkins never visited Montreal or Toronto. He did. He mentions in biographical information that Windsor Station in Montreal, and Spadina Terminal in Toronto made an impression on him. Which is to say that the Folkins family passed through the big cities, possibly never venturing far from the familiar railroad surroundings of stations and terminals, when on their way to some Maritime or small town destination.

Wentworth Folkins was, and remains, a small town person. Even when he later made the decision to move to a big city like Toronto, a move in common with so many others of his generation, eventually joining the faculty of Ryerson, he apparently "broke Toronto down into small-town size" by focusing on the city's neighborhoods. His paintings of "West Toronto Station" and of "Sunnyside Station" are so closely focused that the huge city lurking beyond never intrudes. In his one painting of Toronto's Union Station (in this collection), steam

*The Quebecer* leaving Cochrane, Ontario in the Summer of 1950, with Otty Folkins in charge of CN Pacific class engine #5278.

from the locomotive obscures all but the very top of the Royal York Hotel and lays a smokescreen over the rest of the city's core.

There is a determined denial of the big city, urban drift and technological progress in Wentworth Folkins' work. His focus on steam trains is an anchor that keeps his imagination firmly rooted in small towns the puffing locomotives once served, in a way of life that once was. In the artist's loyalty to "things past" lies an unexpected treasure for us all. His paintings are not really canvases at all. They are mirrors. Magic mirrors. They show us, when we look into them, the way we were ... and, perhaps, the way we should have remained. The world of Wentworth Folkins is "Charlie's World," as he admits clearly enough in his own description of the painting. And it is a world infinitely more poignant than something created from sheer imagination. Imagination can range anywhere. But "Charlie's World," and the world of Wentworth Folkins, has not been spun from the imaginary fabric of anywhere and anywhen, it is firmly rooted in a place, time and reality where we have been ... and to which we can never return.

So, when you browse through the paintings in this book, look first at the steam trains ... it's obligatory ... and then look at the times, places and soul of the world that Folkins' steam locomotives evoke. Take your time. Sooner or later you'll recognize some half-remembered part of yourself taking life in the canvas.

And that's when you should look at the locomotive again. Concentrate on every wheel, piston, connecting rod and rivet. If you don't, you'll find that lump in your throat grow tighter and you'll feel the wetness of tears skittering down your cheeks.

*The Quebecer* leaving Cochrane, Ontario, Christmas 1951, with Wentworth's father, Otty, at the controls.

## THE NEWFIE BULLET, NEWFOUNDLAND 1938

Canada's 10th province and the last to join Confederation, Newfoundland, boasted one of the most legendary steam trains in North America's rich railroading history. Called the "Newfie Bullet" in semi-affection, this nickname for the steam service was something of a back-handed compliment, and there are plenty of Newfie jokes about the time taken to travel from Port aux Basques, the western terminus, to St. John's. Officially, the trip supposedly required 27 hours, but the rugged terrain and gales could, and did, lengthen this considerably. In high winds the train had to be stopped and lashed to the track to keep it from being blown off its narrow-gauge rails. In the winter of 1941, the train was stranded for 17 days in a snowstorm. The Newfie Bullet had an adventurous history, a small island-sized train battling fierce elements and daunting interior grades on its narrow-gauge track across the rocky island.

The line began in St. John's in 1881 and inched slowly westward toward distant Port aux Basques. By 1898 the gandy-dancers had laid all 547 gruelling miles of track across the almost uncharted interior and along the desolate coastline. Originally it was a private line, but over the years the government became more involved in its operation. A well known Canadian railroad contractor, Sir Robert Reid, administered the system until 1949. The railway joined the Canadian National system when Newfoundland "chose Canada," to use the phrase of the equally legendary Joey Smallwood.

Leaving Port aux Basques to begin its hopeful journey towards St. John's the Newfie Bullet passed through tiny towns and outports like Badger, Tickle Harbour, Harry's Brook and Norris Arm. Here, I have chosen to begin my portfolio of 50 Canadian steam trains with a painting of "Newfie Bullet #2" of the Newfoundland Railway, officially designated the "Caribou." I've taken you to a spot along the rugged coast not far out of Port aux Basques where the gallant Newfie Bullet gathers her strength and starts making the turn for her determined thrust inland toward far away St. John's.

## ST. MARGARET'S BAY, NOVA SCOTIA 1944

In 1944, the last year of the war, when I was still a kid, I visited an aunt down east in Nova Scotia. She lived on the "south shore," as Nova Scotians call the coastline west of Halifax, on St. Margaret's Bay. I remember that when I arrived it was nearly dark and my mind was filled with dark fears of a distant war I could not understand. As night fell, the bay seemed an eerie and desolate place because of the blackout. No cozy lights glowed from fisherfolk's cottages in coves around the bay because German subs were known to lurk offshore. My first impression of Nova Scotia was drifting into a restless sleep filled with uneasy shadows of apprehension, half-remembered snatches of threatening dreams.

Then the morning came, suddenly and brightly, not with a rooster's crow, but with the confident, cheerful whistle of #1138 pulling into the village station for its brief stop. The little "Ten Wheeler" (4-6-0) was typical of the type of small locomotive that Canadian National used on branch lines throughout Nova Scotia and the rest of Canada. Locomotive #1138 had been built in 1913 in Montreal for the Canadian Northern Railway and was scrapped in 1961.

But that morning in 1944, for all its modest size and power — and seemingly outsized cheerful whistle — #1138 awakened me to a world of security and normalcy. I looked around and saw the snug little cottages, the colourful fishing boats bobbing at their moorings, piles of lobster traps on weathered wharves, and the soaring white gulls flashing silver in the rising sun, and the brilliant bright blue waters of St. Margaret's Bay studded with sun-dappled islets and secret coves.

Old #1138 and its colleagues are no more. Daily passenger rail service between Halifax and Yarmouth, which once stopped at all the small communities gathered on the shore of St. Margaret's Bay, has been discontinued. The magic of the steam train has been erased by a new generation of superhighways following the coast. The old rail lines are now lanes of weeds meandering meaninglessly through the trees at the heads of coves, and the creosoted trestle is slowly collapsing into Five Island Lake.

## AUTO CAMP GROUND, NOVA SCOTIA 1925

One day as I was digging through old family photographs for a painting theme, I came across some yellowed and wiggly-edged "kodaks" of auto camping scenes involving my parents and their first car. And looking at the pictures brought to life the stories they told about their early motoring adventures. In those days it was an arduous adventure to reach the Maritimes, or even southern Ontario, from my parents' home in Cochrane. In fact, back in 1925, Cochrane didn't even have a road connection to the south, and the fragile autos of the time had to suffer the indignity of riding the rails to North Bay. From there it was 2 days of hard driving even to reach Montreal or Toronto. The Maritimes were a hopeful 4 more days along rutted roads. Back then, of course, motels were an innovative idea in the minds of those who actually had faith in the future of the automobile and the drivers and passengers of the era simply stopped wherever fatigue, darkness or mechanical misadventure befell them. Until motels began to dot the highways at convenient intervals, the "auto camp" was as much a part of long-distance driving as cranking the starter in the morning (when the new-fangled battery and electric starter had succumbed to the night's dew). In this scene, I've shown my family actually making it to the Maritimes. It was somewhere near Truro, Nova Scotia, at sunrise when they were awakened, and the dog thrown into a frenzy, by the steam-blast of #1138 roaring out of the mist along the nearby railroad tracks. Such power, magnificence, confidence! And the auto-campers looked blearily through dis-coloured isinglass "auto curtains" (windows) and climbed from beneath the variety of interesting "auto-tents" they had managed to contrive, and began the chore of making breakfast. Speeding past, with a comfortable night's sleep behind them in their berths, and enjoying breakfast in the dining car, passengers behind #1138 probably smiled at their fleeting glimpse of disheveled auto campers piling out of their flimsy vehicles.

## THE WATER STOP, NEW BRUNSWICK
## 1935

Find a steam locomotive and you'll usually find a boy close by, so as you'll notice in my portfolio I've often realistically included small boys, barking dogs (or both) just as Renaissance painters realistically portrayed lap dogs on the velvet skirts of their clients! In my imagination, the urchin sitting beside the tracks is "Jeff" and he was on his way to his favourite fishing hole before being entranced by the spectacle of #29 American-type 4-4-0 locomotive shuffling to a halt for a drink of water.

The locomotive pictured here, #29, was built in 1887 by Canadian Pacific along lines engineered in America for locomotives intended for medium-length hauls in regions where water was plentiful and where grades were not too steep, loads not too large. A "general service" type of locomotive in eastern North America, locomotives like #29 watered frequently every day throughout rural New Brunswick, Nova Scotia, Prince Edward Island, Ontario and Quebec. As boys watched...

This particular locomotive, #29, was saved from scrapping by the Canadian Railroad Historical Association and until recently was part of the collection at Delson, Quebec. Now #29 has been loaned to a new steam excursion operation, but as a static display, at Hillsboro, New Brunswick. One of the last steam locomotives to run on the Canadian Pacific system, in service as late as 1960, I've heard rumours that #29 may become active again and has been steam-tested to determine her capabilities.

## NUMBER 136 IN NEW BRUNSWICK 1952

Rusty and more than a little work-worn after 77 years of service this grand old lady went on to become a TV star.

Here we see #136 rolling down the line between Chipman and Norton, New Brunswick, back in 1952, as the afternoon sun casts long shadows over this peaceful land of elm and maple trees.

This classic locomotive, an American type, 4-4-0, was still based in New Brunswick with two other sisters, #29 and #144 when steam power finally retired in 1960. Early in the 1970s, after years of disuse and storage in an old barn near Bolton, Ontario, the newly formed Ontario Rail Association undertook the complete rebuilding of #136. By 1973 she was ready for action and headed west to star in the filming of Pierre Berton's C.B.C. Television history of the Canadian Pacific, "*The National Dream.*"

Built by the Rogers Locomotive Works in 1883, she was 2 years old before the last spike was driven to complete the Canadian Pacific Railway.

Presently, #136 is stored at Tottenham, Ontario, along with #1057. Once the new steam excursion line being set up by the Ontario Rail Foundation and the Town of Tottenham is opened, #136 will once again strut her stuff through a landscape much like we see her in here.

## PRINCE EDWARD ISLAND 1930

Prince Edward Island! So many things come to mind! The surrounding sea and its bountiful harvest. Rich, red deep earth and its unceasing production of potatoes, potatoes! Anne of Green Gables. Tiny villages and small towns nestled in dells between rounded hills, or in sheltered arms of the sea. A neat, tiny and perfect place.

When I finally visited our smallest province, I discovered that Prince Edward Island had once had a neat, tiny, perfect railway. Many communities had long existed on the island before a narrow gauge railway line was begun in the 1870s. Being such a small province, the railway was not desperately needed and for a long time the Shire-sized trains struggled to justify their existence. In fact, one of Prince Edward Island's conditions for entering Confederation in 1873 included Federal Government participation in their railway system. In spite of the difficulties, P.E.I. narrow gauge trains continued to operate for many years. The little teapot working up steam in my painting, locomotive #34, pulled the last narrow gauge passenger train into Charlottetown in 1930. At that time, the gauge was changed to standard but steam locomotives continued to work the larger system until the 1950s. Today diesel locomotives handle any freight that moves and is interchanged with the mainland, but there is no longer any rail passenger service on the island.

My painting doesn't depict any particular location. The scene is my idea of the essence of P.E.I. A kindly sun warms a village with its clapboard houses gathered around the local church, just as it warms the tilled, rich earth that will bring the autumn's harvest of potatoes. A kid on the bridge marvels at the forms of strange marine creatures temporarily stranded in pools of the little tidal river, while a calm, pipe-smoking farmer looks on the scene in the knowledge that basic things must endure. Within this scene, I think, the tiny teapot locomotive, #34, belongs more than the throbbing, muscled diesels ever will.

## WINDSOR STATION, MONTREAL, QUEBEC 1939

There's plenty of noise at the west end of Montreal's Windsor Station on a summer evening in 1939 at 11 P.M. One of Canadian Pacific's big "Northern Types" (4-8-4), #3100, blasts into action with billows of smoke and steam preparing for her high-speed night run to Toronto.

Canadian Pacific, unlike Canadian National, had only two Northern Type locomotives on its roster, and these were used almost exclusively to pull CP night trains, #21 and #22, between Montreal and Toronto. An obvious feature of CP's Northern Types was the large front end smoke deflector that remained unchanged until these powerful steam locomotives were replaced by diesels in 1952.

Both CP Northerners were preserved at the end of steam in Canada. Locomotive #3100, shown here, is presently in the National Transport Museum in Ottawa, while the other Northern is on display in Saskatchewan.

During the 1930s and 40s, Montreal's Windsor Station was always a major attraction for me whenever my father took me to visit my grandmother in Notre Dame de Grace ... and no wonder, since Windsor Station then boasted 70 steam arrivals and departures a day! Also, my father had awed me with the story of the runaway locomotive that had charged right through the station, jumped the rails and ran through the concourse and a waiting room, ending up hanging through a wall over the street. With 70 arrivals and departures a day, there was always the chance that this spectacle might happen again.

Windsor Station, opened on February 1, 1889, was designed by Bruce Price of New York and reflected his castle-like residential architecture. Later, Bush-designed train sheds with skylights set the station apart from its contemporaries in Europe and in other parts of North America. These were greatly appreciated by crews loading and servicing trains during Montreal's winters. These protective skylights over working areas were removed during World War II as a precaution against flying glass if Montreal were ever subjected to an air raid. Unfortunately, after the war these skylights were never replaced and Windsor Station lost much of its distinctive character.

## "DAILY EVENT," QUEBEC 1934

South of Montreal, near the Quebec-Vermont border, we're right on time to catch "the daily event." Canadian Pacific's Boston-bound train steams into a scene of winter sunshine and plows through newly-fallen snow. The "Alouette" is on schedule.

The old flavour of Quebec's rural Eastern Townships is reflected in this scene of the rugged mountains, the covered bridge and the horse and sleigh. Youngsters interrupt their favourite sport, ice hockey, to wave at today's Alouette and perhaps some budding Rocket Richards fleetingly dream of playing for Les Canadiens on the ice of far away, almost unimaginable Boston ... they have listened to games, and have heard of Boston, on the radio. But only the daily passage of the Alouette assures them that Boston is a reality. In this scene, the Christmas holidays are nearly over and the ice-covered pond has seen continuous action since early Christmas morning when new skates, new hockey sticks and new pucks began to scar its cold, smooth surface. For only continual practice can make the dream real, as real as the Alouette that daily proclaims that there is another world beyond the mountains. There *is* a Boston!

The locomotive, a light Pacific Type (4-6-2), #2229, pulling this day's Alouette was only 21 years old in 1934 and served for another 27 years before being replaced by diesels on this run. Built by Canadian Pacific in Montreal, #2229 was probably more typical of this company's thousands of steam locomotives than many of the larger and more powerful steam locomotives built just before the advent of the diesels. I was happy to find that these Pacific Types worked the daily Boston-bound Alouette as far as Wells River, Vermont because little #2229 seems to fit so well into this rural Quebec scene.

## LAURENTIAN SKI TRAIN, QUEBEC 1944

Throughout the first half of the Century, skiers from Montreal commuted to the Laurentians north of the city on special ski trains scheduled regularly each winter by both the Canadian National and the Canadian Pacific Railways.

Thousands of Montrealers can still recall the ski trains which took them to their favourite slopes. Many friends were made and many a romance had its start on these funny old trains of crowded wooden coaches with their green plush seats, iron stoves and oil lamps. The windows were usually coated with half an inch of ice, so to see out, one had to blow a hole, then quickly peer out before it refroze.

On a typical winter morning in 1944 a Canadian National ski train nears it's destination. Early birds already on the slopes, gaze eagerly at the train as it rolls in bearing more friends. Another memorable week-end is underway.

By Sunday evening, old #5579, a light Pacific, 4-6-2, built in 1911 by the Grand Trunk will be on hand to wheel her train full of happy, exhausted friends back to the city.

#5579 will return again next week, next month and next year until the mid 1950s. By the time diesels replaced steam, the automobile on the new Autoroute had relegated the ski train to just a pleasant memory.

## "SO WHO NEEDS A RAILWAY?"... PICTON, ONTARIO 1925

Well, I for one needed a railway in order to paint this impression of Picton as it was in 1925. The track is still there, but no trains to speak of use it today.

Not long ago, I was enjoying the view from a kitchen window of a friend's 150-year-old house in Picton. The light, the trees and the charming old architecture seemed perfect for a painting and it didn't take long for this one to take shape.

"So who needs a railway?" cried opponents to railroad proposals when progressive souls suggested the idea in the 1870s. The proposition seemed ridiculous to most people, especially considering that Prince Edward County, of which Picton is the largest town, is a peninsula that juts out into Lake Ontario and is almost completely surrounded by water. Furthermore, the years between 1869 and 1890 were known as "the Barley Years" when millions of tons of barley were shipped across the lake by schooner to supply the American distilling industry. The early 1870s were just the beginning of this prosperous schooner-transported boom economy and, human nature being what it is, few could imagine that the demand for barley might ever taper off. A railway ... unless it could be laid on a causeway across Lake Ontario ... seemed absurd.

Nonetheless, there were at least some influential men who foresaw that the barley boom could not last forever and that, when it failed, Prince Edward County's peninsular character made it remote from the east-west pattern of Canadian trade between Montreal and Toronto. They argued that a spur line to the Canadian mainstream was crucial to the county's future growth and prosperity. A rail line was laid in 1879 called "The Prince Edward County Railway," by 1909 it had been taken over by Canadian Northern and in 1923 it was absorbed into the newly formed Canadian National system. By then, the tracks had been extended north of the original terminus at Trenton to service the mining country a bit further north.

The "Ten Wheeler" I have depicted, #1027, was originally built for the line in 1907 by the Kingston Locomotive Works and served for exactly 20 years before being scrapped. This is probably its only painted portrait.

## OTTAWA UNION STATION, ONTARIO
## 1953

Arriving at this station one bright August morning in 1944, I remember the excitement of my first sight of the Peace Tower and the Chateau Laurier. We walked on Rideau Street, right in the heart of downtown Ottawa, in the time we had before re-boarding our train for Montreal.

This station was opened on June 1st, 1912. Originally, the station and the Chateau Laurier were built by the Grand Trunk Railway to blend architecturally with existing Government buildings.

In later years the station became a Union Station accepting the arrival and departure of Canadian Pacific and New York Central trains as well as Canadian National.

Sadly it was decided to close the Station and open a new one 2 miles from the city centre in July, 1966. Saved from demolition, this old Station was renovated and reopened as a Government Conference Centre in 1969.

To my surprise, I discovered during a recent visit that this view including the Parliament Buildings, the Chateau and the old Union Station has changed very little. Trainsheds, tracks and trains have been replaced by walkways, landscaping and roads. Canadian Pacific's trim little Pacific Type passenger locomotive #1201 doesn't frequent the neighbourhood anymore, but she's still very much alive and operating in the Ottawa area.

Following the demise of steam in 1960, #1201, the last steam locomotive ever built in Canadian Pacific's own Angus Shops in Montreal, was saved by Museums Canada, overhauled and runs regularly during the summer months. Its regular haunt is the Canadian Pacific branchline up the Gatineau to Wakefield, Quebec, but a few years ago, I watched her performance in Vancouver during Expo 86.

29

## MUSKOKA WHARF, ONTARIO 1934

Within living memory, travel and vacationing in the lake district of Southern Ontario depended on a proud fleet of wooden steamboats that plied the waters of the Muskokas, Lake Couchiching and Lake Simcoe, and the sparkling Kawarthas. And, half a century ago, a network of spur-line railroads carried steam-powered trains to the wharves where the lake steamers docked. These romantic and colourful steamboats, like the trains themselves, have vanished.

But once, not really so long ago, transfer points for steam trains and steamboats flourished at a number of locations: Bala, Burk's Falls, Gravenhurst and Lakefield. At these lakeside junctions, boats and trains exchanged vacation-eager passengers, freight and mail. At Gravenhurst on Lake Muskoka, the Grand Trunk Railway built a substantial wharf and railway station. Trains from Toronto, including the legendary summertime "Muskoka Express," carried vacationing families within feet of waiting steamboats. The white vessels eased away from the wharf, swung slowly out into the lake, and puffed and churned across the water to deposit their passengers at large vacation resorts that then dotted the shores of all the sparkling lakes.

But with the beginning of the Great Depression in 1929, the era of carefree vacations came to an end for many people. An end to the colourful lake steamboats was in sight and never returned. The prosperity of the 1950s led to the purchase of private cottages. Highways and secondary roads inched their way into every nook, cove and cranny along the shores of every popular lake. The railroad wharves and the steamboat docks were abandoned and hardly a trace of them remains today.

Through the efforts of some helpful Gravenhurst citizens, the Gravenhurst library and publications like *The Steamboat Era in the Muskokas* by Richard Tatley, plus a visit to the derelict wharf, I was able to develop this painting. I have shown Muskoka Wharf on a summertime late afternoon ... and late in its active life. Locomotive #5112 of Canadian National backs slowly along the wharf to couple with its train, the "Muskoka Express," about to return sunburned vacationers to Toronto. The steamboats *Segwun* and *Sagamo*, loaded with passengers just delivered by the incoming "Muskoka Express" prepare to ease out into the lake.

## ALGONQUIN PARK STATION, ONTARIO 1935

One more excursion train puffs slowly into the little Grand Trunk station at Algonquin Park, all passengers eager for fresh air and sunshine, happy to have escaped from the steaming cities. Soon, these new arrivals will join those already canoeing, hiking and fishing in Ontario's huge provincial park. The Grand Trunk Railway mounted highly successful publicity campaigns attracting vacationers to Algonquin Park as far back as 1905, shortly after taking over the line.

But early in the 1930s a new highway into the park began to drain away railway profits. By 1935 the line, which once stretched from Depot Harbour on Lake Huron all the way to Ottawa, was closed east of Algonquin Park and reverted to its older role of short-hauling timber, grain and iron ore to supplement the decline in vacationing passengers. By 1957 Canadian National, which had taken over the railway from the old Grand Trunk consortium, could no longer sustain the financial losses being suffered by the Highland Inn located at the station in Algonquin Park and had the Edwardian hotel demolished. The "end of the line" came finally in 1959 when passenger rail service to Algonquin Park was discontinued.

I have depicted Algonquin Park Station, and the Highland Inn directly behind it, in their heyday... but with twilight not far off. Canadian National's venerable old Mogul Type (2-6-0) locomotive #674 served the vacation run in 1935, a year when there was still plenty of passenger traffic but also when the impact of the new highway was impossible to ignore. This was the year that the railway was closed east of Algonquin Park, so there will not be much track left in front of #674 when she finally hisses to a stop.

Today, hardly a trace remains of this Algonquin Park resort of the steam era while once it throbbed with life year round.

## "GONE FISHING," ONTARIO 1936

A steam-powered mixed train on a timber trestle, an old rusty steel truss highway bridge, a Model A Ford and some children fishing should recall to many the 1920s and 30s when the world seemed a little less complicated.

Smell the moist early morning air as the sun slowly burns away the mist hiding our view of the river. Listen to the occasional call of a blue jay or cardinal. Suddenly the spell is broken by the advance of one of Canadian Pacifics familiar D10's-#1057, as it rumbles onto the trestle hauling its train of freight and passenger cars. From his vantage point, the engineer has a great view of life along the line, as he makes his twice-weekly run through this part of western Ontario.

In 1960, as steam was retired from the Canadian Pacific Railway, #1057 was saved from the scrapper's torch by a rail enthusiast who later sold it to the Ontario Rail Association. During the early 1970s, #1057, along with another C.P. locomotive-#136 hauled numerous rail excursions to Orangeville and Owen Sound.

Presently #1057 and #136 are located in Tottenham, Ontario awaiting the set up and completion of a new Steam excursion line being organized by the Ontario Rail Foundation in co-operation with the Town of Tottenham. The new line will utilize a few miles of the old Canadian National, Hamilton to Allendale and Collingwood main line which has been abandoned for years. Due to the character of the countryside through which this new line will operate we may once again experience scenes like "Gone Fishing."

## "CHARLIE'S WORLD," ONTARIO 1946

It seemed to me that Charlie could read almost as soon as he started to walk. Of course, his parents gave him all those kid's word-picture books as soon as he could toddle. And then adventure books with more words than pictures, and finally books with plenty of words and almost no pictures at all. Charlie's books were always about things past. Pirates and princes. Elves and enchantments. Charlie never bothered to read comics, and I'm sure he never got into anything about trains.

But we liked having Charlie around. Although he wasn't very good at building things himself, he had ideas about things that the rest of us could build. We discovered this swell spot near the railroad tracks where an old tree overhung the creek. It was a great spot for swimming and a lookout in the tree could warn us of any sisters sneaking up to peek and giggle. It was Charlie's idea to use the old wood lying around to make a proper tree-house, and we did. And it was Charlie's idea to use a pile of old railroad ties to make a raft. I guess, for Charlie, the tree-house wasn't just a tree-house the way us other kids saw it. It was a castle in the air where he could think and dream about past things he read in books. And for him, I think, our raft was a pirate ship with silk sails that could explore a creek whose horizons were far wider than its banks.

That's Stephen, waving to the engineer just as old #914 ambles into view with a mixed local. The old CN Mogul is taking its train from Palmerston to Kincardine, like it does every couple of days. The other boys would be waving too, but I guess they're all under water keeping cool . . . and too shy to get out. Charlie never paid any attention to old #914. He's up in the tree-house, wrapped in his world, and it doesn't include anything as exciting and modern as the CN Mogul.

Whatever became of Charlie? Well, he grew up and I heard that he went to university. Just recently somebody told me that he was now a world authority on steam propulsion.

## THE DON STATION, TORONTO, ONTARIO 1949

This small but well known old Toronto station was built in 1899 as a stop on the Toronto Belt Line. It was purchased in 1901 by the Canadian Pacific but later used by both Canadian Pacific and Canadian National. It's original location was on the west bank of the Don River just below Queen Street. In later years the Don station finally earned a quiet retirement location at Todmorden Mills Pioneer Village.

More than 50 trains a day would pass this station as it was on the mainline of the two major railroads. Trains such as "The Northland," "The Continental Limited," and Canadian Pacific's #21 and #22, were daily visitors.

Early one spring morning in 1949, almost before sun-up, a few rail fans were on hand to watch the action as two Canadian National freights worked through the station. On the head end of the northbound freight was another of C.N.s Mikado Type, 2-8-2, freight locomotives. The engineer's mind is on the long grade to Oriole up the Don Valley as he slows slightly to pick up his orders on the fly from the operator. As he opens the throttle, one young fan finds the roar of the exhaust and the blast of the whistle too much, so he plugs his ears with his fingers. His old friend, perhaps not quite so sensitive to the sounds, is relishing his pipe and the old familiar scene.

## THE RAILROAD CHILDREN, TORONTO, ONTARIO 1928

Hundreds of back yards throughout Toronto and many other Canadian cities have a railway right-of-way, or a rail yard, rather than a back lane, to face onto. A conspicuous example of such an arrangement is the right-of-way across Toronto running through Forest Hill and Chaplin Estates. This was originally called "the Belt Line," and anyone who has heard of these residential areas knows that they are not on "the wrong side of the tracks." Coming from a small northern town where the railway serviced only what might be called the "business section," when I moved to Toronto I was fascinated by the trains that could be seen in some of my friends' back yards.

Unfortunately, my own back yard does not boast this feature but the possibility of a painting on this back yard theme had been on my mind for some time. One day in the early 1970s our neighbours' three children were in clear view from one of our second storey windows. Anna, Barbara and Charlie (remember him?) were having a wonderful time playing in the tree-house their father had helped them make from the remains of the worn out garage.

The whole composition needed a focus and, in my imagination, this rolled down the track in the form of one of Canadian National's diminutive (0-6-0) yard switchers, #7332, complete with its engineer who was obviously well known to the children. Thousands of switchers like #7332 were built by Canadian Foundry around 1915 and worked the yards of North America with little recognition of their valuable contribution to railroading. So I thought it fitting that the memory of at least one should be preserved even though #7332 was scrapped in 1957.

## NORTH TORONTO STATION, ONTARIO 1925

At 10:30 P.M. on a cool September evening in 1925 we are standing to the northeast, at track level, in North Toronto Station. Trains are being switched and passengers are boarding a westbound special just as the clock strikes the time of departure in the great tower. Locomotive #2302 is eastbound for Montreal.

North Toronto Station was built in less than a year during World War I. It was active for nearly 15 years and then abandoned during the Great Depression in 1930. During its career it welcomed visiting royalty as well as serving the travelling needs of ordinary Canadians. The Prince of Wales and Prince George were greeted here in the 1920s. The station was re-opened for one day in the spring of 1939 for the arrival of King George VI and Queen Elizabeth during the Toronto stop of their cross-Canada tour.

The station has survived the years, even though it is now used as a liquor store and even though its once magnificent clock has been removed from the tower. But we can still admire its neo-Classic lines and detail. In essence this fine old Toronto landmark is intact.

## BATHURST STREET, TORONTO, ONTARIO 1942

Night after night all through World War II, huge wartime freight trains were assembled in Canadian National's Mimico yard. Thousands of tons of war material destined, eventually, for Canada's East Coast ports for trans-shipment across the Atlantic. From Mimico to the Scarborough heights, the railway grade was all uphill and to get the massive freight trains moving demanded exceptional power ... even though the run in terms of mere mileage was fairly short. Invariably, one of C.N.'s five powerful, ponderous, Santa Fe Type (2-10-2) freight transfer locomotives would double-head each long train of heavily loaded rolling stock as far as Scarborough. Then, when the Santa Fe Types had topped the Scarborough crest so that a smaller locomotive could manage the grades further east, they sped back to Mimico to be ready for the next night's gruelling test of power and traction.

Here, passengers aboard a Peter Witt-designed streetcar of the Toronto Transit Commission are treated, on this wet winter night, to a view of Santa Fe #4101 surging under the Bathurst Street bridge. For it is here, at the convergence of Toronto Terminal tracks and main lines, at the throat of the railway yard, that the brutal eastward climb begins. The passengers on the streetcar witness the great billow of smoke and steam that *cannot quite* obscure the ruddy glow of power from the Santa Fe's boiler. The engineer has just opened the throttle feeding pressurized steam to giant pistons and drive wheels, releasing 80,000 pounds of brute tractive power in answer to the eastern grade up to Scarborough. Another long and immensely heavy train of freight cars will not falter on its climb up the Scarborough Bluffs.

I have depicted this leading Santa Fe locomotive, #4101, in sooty grey olive drab as befits a working warhorse toiling tirelessly during the urgency of 1942. A world, and a way of life, hung in the balance of nightly struggles like this one, and it was no time for the arrogance of bright and normal company colours.

## "THE INTERNATIONAL" STEAM SPECTACULAR, TORONTO, ONTARIO 1931

One of Canadian National's most famous trains, "The International Ltd.," was scheduled to leave Toronto's Union Station daily at 9:15 A.M. during almost three decades, from the 1930s well into the 1950s. "The International" was usually pulled by one of the railway's huge, powerful, high-speed "Northern Type" (4-8-4) U2 class locomotives.

On a bright, cool summer morning in 1931, the Northern Type U2 class locomotive #6123 presents a spectacular sight as the engineer opens her throttle, unleashing thousands of horsepower, to set "The International" in motion. Destination — Montreal.

At the close of World War II there were 203 Northerns on Canadian National's steam roster. Shortly before the war European-style smoke deflectors were installed on all C.N. Northerns then in service. The deflectors tended to enhance their massive appearance, but even without them the Northerns still looked very impressive.

It is interesting to note that in 1931, the date in which I have set this composition, the locomotive, the station and the Royal York Hotel are all less than 4 years old.

## SUNNYSIDE STATION, TORONTO, ONTARIO
### 1935

"Meet me at Sunnyside" was a Torontonian invitation to fun and friendship. Located on the south side of one of Toronto's busiest intersections where King and Queen Streets met at the foot of Roncesvalles Avenue, this popular tourist area and amusement park is another Toronto landmark lost to progress.

Although the station and railway lines through Sunnyside were Canadian National, trains of the Canadian Pacific and Toronto Hamilton and Buffalo used them through a long standing agreement reached late in the 19th century.

Day and night, famous trains such as "The International Limited," "The Maple Leaf," "The Inter-City Limited" and "The Forest City" stopped at Sunnyside for the convenience of West-enders.

In this morning scene, Buffalo-bound Canadian Pacific train #721 rolls in. Passengers on business and some on holiday board for destinations in the United States, New York, Pittsburg, Cleveland and Rochester. Up in front of the station a couple of train watchers enjoy the activity.

Canadian Pacific at this time had four locomotives known as C.P.'s International locomotives. Pacific, #2715, here on #721, was one of these equipped with Automatic Train Control equipment necessary for any locomotive running into Buffalo on New York Central Lines. In 1938, #2715 was replaced and sent to western Canada to join 17 others of her class operating into Vancouver.

"Meet me at Sunnyside" has lost its meaning for Torontonians. The amusement park went first to accommodate an expressway and then the station built in 1912 was demolished in the late 1960s.

## WEST TORONTO STATION, ONTARIO
## 1930

West Toronto Station, located at the intersection of Dundas and Annette streets, was a very active place in Toronto's West End during the 20th century's "Golden Age" of steam travel.

Built in 1911, it replaced a smaller station located north of the rail junction. Not many stations of this individualistic period were similar to each other, but West Toronto Station happened to closely resemble in size and architecture the Canadian Pacific station in London, Ontario.

Many famous Canadian Pacific passenger trains stopped regularly at West Toronto Station: "The Trans Canada Limited," "The Royal York," "The Dominion" and "The Canadian." Here, in 1930, "The Trans Canada Limited" (sleeping car passengers only) is easing to a halt. The well-dressed lady is here to meet her relatives coming in from Vancouver, while her son lingers lovingly over their new Model "A" Ford. The chauffeur is on hand to meet his incoming employer with the Chrysler Town Car. In 1930, everything of importance pertaining to either domestic or business travel focused on railway stations and trains.

The well proportioned structure and characteristic details of West Toronto Station suffered little from "renovation" over the years, but it gradually fell into disuse in the late 1960s and early 1970s as the volume of passenger rail travel declined all over North America.

Early one November morning in 1982, Toronto learned that it no longer had a West Toronto Station. The building had been demolished before dawn by a C.P.R. wrecking crew. Another of Toronto's historic buildings had disappeared. It was 71 years old.

This painting is a reflection of a memorable time in Toronto's past.

## "SIR HENRY'S TIME MACHINE," WHITBY, ONTARIO 1931

Only minutes from its destination, Toronto's Union Station, and determined not to be even a few seconds late, Canadian National's train #15, the famed "International," roars through Whitby, Ontario. There's not even a thought that this magnificent flagship train will pause at such an inconsequential whistle-stop station! The new Hudson Type high-speed passenger locomotive (4-6-4) sends hats, newspapers and frightened dogs flying in the wind and roar of its passage.

In 1930, train #15, the "International" was running between Montreal and Toronto in a little more than 6 hours. Canadian National's President, Sir Henry Thornton, thought that the time could be reduced to 5½ hours with a more powerful locomotive. Accordingly Sir Henry authorized the building of five newly-designed Hudson Types by the Montreal Locomotive Works. The first three were delivered in 1930, and by 1931 everyone realized that Sir Henry was on the right track. The Hudsons made the Toronto-Montreal run in just 5½ hours. Here, Hudson #5700 rips through Whitby station leaving a modest hurricane in its wake ... a real time machine.

Sir Henry Thornton was originally an American, a genius at dealing with railway problems. He had been knighted for his managerial contributions to Britain's Great Eastern railroad. He became the first President of the newly-formed Canadian National Railway in 1923, inheriting a company debt of $1.3 *billion*. Within a year he had erased the debt and earned an operating surplus of $18 million. Much has been written about Sir Henry's accomplishments with the early Canadian National, and no writer has overlooked the genuine esteem and popularity with which the company's employees viewed him. Unfortunately, the esteem and respect were not shared by the politicians who controlled his future.

## "HOME FOR CHRISTMAS," ONTARIO 1937

Some winters have been extremely severe in southwestern Ontario, and in particular the winter of 1947 which was the subject of an earlier painting. But the winter exactly a decade earlier was not much kinder. Even severe winter weather can be quite inspiring for some artists.

Blizzards and mountainous drifts of snow invariably generate feelings of concern and mild anxiety. As Christmas approaches, this underlying worry of a severe winter somehow brings people closer together in the realization of their common vulnerability to nature and the necessity to co-operate cheerfully, and work a bit harder, if life is to continue normally. Season's greetings are a touch more genuine during a severe winter, homecomings are measurably warmer. Thanks are more heartfelt. Blessings more truly appreciated.

So it is that in spite of the heavy snow, a festive mood surrounds the arrival of a Canadian National "Ten Wheeler," #1532, at this tiny rural station. Although we cannot see them from this angle, we can imagine the cozy old wooden coaches spilling their happy homecoming passengers onto the platform and into the waiting arms of loved ones.

"All aboard!" Even the baggage-cart handler pulls his burden with jaunty, joyful purpose, and the man waving to the engineer conveys a little more respect and affection than usual. Little #1532 noses into the blinding snow heading toward her next stop with her remaining passengers, and more loving homecomings down the line.

Although this scene is typical of a specific period, the warmth of homecoming — especially during a hard winter at Christmas — is timeless. The station depicted here once stood on the main street of Hickson, Ontario.

## SEPTEMBER AFTERNOON, ONTARIO 1948

This adventure concerns three boys on a raft, a scenario reminiscent of Mark Twain's, Tom, Huck and Jim ... but I have in mind the eternal Charlie, Stephen and one of the other boys navigating their tree-shaded swimming hole. It is early September in southern Ontario and school should be their main concern, but the sun is warm and the surroundings inspire one more adventure before submission to a fall and winter of close encounters. Perhaps they will escape into Charlie's make-believe world of pirates cruising a tropical sea or Mutiny on the Bounty. Their adventure will reach such vast dimensions that its bounds will only be limited by their imagination.

    Momentarily their spell is broken. An aging Canadian Pacific (0-6-0) switch engine rumbles into the scene as it rolls across the old wooden trestle from one side of the little valley to the other. The train crew will perhaps be reminded of their days of adventure in the valley long ago.

    By 1958 the steam switcher had been scrapped, replaced by a little diesel, but other generations of pirates would cruise this swimming hole with just as fantastic imaginations. Trains would occasionally interrupt the spell.

## THE WINTER OF 1947, ONTARIO

Some of us will remember that the winter of 1947 turned out to be one of the worst on record for western Ontario. Trains leaving Palmerston for Kincardine, Southampton, Wiarton, Owen Sound and Durham were delayed for days. Steam-powered plows and hundreds of men battled mountainous drifts of snow in an attempt to keep the rail lines clear.

Here is a scene typical of that terrible winter. A Canadian National "Consolidated Type" freight locomotive, #2190, churns, slowly past the old Grand Trunk station where men struggle to shovel away the drifts. Locomotive #2190 has just replenished its water from the heated, wood-sheathed water tank. Hours of plowing through drifting snow, with #2190's wheels slipping on icy track, lay ahead for this train crew.

Locomotive #2190, a M-3-c Class Consolidation Type (2-8-0) was originally built by the Montreal Locomotive Works for Canadian Government Railways as #211 in 1913. By 1923 when #2190 became one of the newly formed Canadian Nationals total of 3,256 steam locomotives, the railway had 779 Consolidation locomotives. By 1947, #2190 was one of 616 Consolidations. They still accounted for a large proportion of the locomotives in service, and they still were very necessary in keeping all the little towns and villages in Canada in communication.

## TORONTO, HAMILTON & BUFFALO STATION, HAMILTON, ONTARIO
## 1939

A warm summer evening in 1939. The Toronto, Hamilton and Buffalo Railways' Toronto-to-Buffalo evening train stops briefly at Hamilton's new T.H. & B. downtown station. Reflecting the latest Art Deco trends in architecture, the modern concrete, glass and stainless steel structure complements the equally fine and modern mechanical proportions of locomotive #15, a "Pacific Type." Built by the Montreal Locomotive Works in 1923, #15 was one of two modern Pacific Types used on this run. But tomorrow the same train might arrive behind a Canadian Pacific "Hudson Type" or behind a New York Central "Pacific Type." T.H. & B. was a railway owned jointly by C.P. and New York Central.

Referred to in railroading terms as a "bridge line," T.H. & B. connected the track systems of its two parent companies, running from Buffalo to Hamilton but with rail-usage rights all the way to Toronto over the Canadian National main line.

Canadian Pacific recently acquired complete control of T.H. & B., and this little railroad company has ceased to exist. But its Art Deco station still stands in downtown Hamilton. Although not used for many years this station may someday be recommissioned to serve the community.

## INGLEWOOD, ONTARIO
## 1939

When the Canadian Pacific and Canadian National converged on this location in the 1870s, the place was called Sligo Junction. It became Riverdale in 1883, and finally Inglewood when some confusion arose in the Post Office because of Toronto's Riverdale community.

Inglewood was not a large town even in 1939, but like many Ontario communities it prospered quietly for many years after the railroads established reliable transportation for its products. Inglewood had a modest woolen industry and several quarry businesses. Larger centres, like Hamilton and Toronto nearby, were a continuously growing market for clothing textiles and building stone.

I've pictured Inglewood station on a summer's day in 1939. Just after the King and Queen had paid the Dominion a lengthy visit which was still a topic of animated conversation... and just before the world would be plunged into turmoil in September, which was a topic of concerned speculation as war clouds gathered over Europe. But for the moment, as brief as it is, Inglewood is at peace and is proud to have a "union station," serviced by both C.P. and C.N. The Canadian National trains through Inglewood ran from Hamilton to Allendale, while the Canadian Pacific trains ran from Toronto and on to Orangeville and Owen Sound. Not the centre of the world, perhaps, Inglewood was nonetheless well-connected during the era of steam railways. I have depicted the *second* Inglewood railway station, the one built around 1910 and which was demolished as a derelict building in the 1970s.

An old Canadian Pacific "Ten Wheeler," #434, rolls slowly over the diamond after taking on water. I fancy that the man in the white suit is a travelling salesman, a quarry or textile representative, waiting to board for Toronto or Hamilton and secure in the expectation of reasonable profit and comfortable living. This may well be his last sales trip under such carefree circumstances. Within weeks the Nazis will invade Poland, the textile industry will come under government regulation, and much planned construction will be curtailed for the duration.

## WINTER NIGHT, INGLEWOOD, ONTARIO 1948

A stormy winter night like this is a nightmare for the men responsible for keeping the tracks open and the trains moving. The mechanical devices they depend on so completely in normal weather — switches, signals, air pumps and generators — just refuse to function. Forget about schedules. Just keep the trains moving if possible, make sure that no train is stranded if possible ... and make damned sure there's no collision because of frozen switches on the line!

Thank God, she made it. There she is, C.N. #5606 just crossing the diamond with the local. She was due more than four hours ago, but must have had a rough time in those cuts near Caledon East and Palgrave.

Once the C.N. local clears the diamond, will C.P. (left) chance it up to Orangeville, or will they hold her until morning? It would be a rough run, all upgrade, for the D-4 #454 to Orangeville, even with a small freight to pull. But it's Hobson's Choice ... the whole train could just as well be snowed in right here in the station.

## TOTTENHAM, ONTARIO
## 1931

It's "business as usual" on this bright autumn morning back in 1931 at Tottenham. The village's Grand Trunk Station, built before the turn of the century, receives a little artistic attention. A local farmer suspects that his truck isn't as spunky as she should be and takes a look under the hood before driving back to the farm with a few bags of feed.

Everyone in Tottenham is "laid back," as we would say nowadays, and there's no reason to be otherwise. Even the engineer of locomotive #915, an old Canadian National E-10-a, Mogul Type (2-6-0), seems in no hurry to leave the siding for his next stop down the line. Mogul #915 was built in 1910 by the Canadian Locomotive Works in Kingston, Ontario, one of 25 in its class. Originally built for the Grand Trunk Railway as #1000, this locomotive, was later numbered #902, then #915 and finally #80 in 1951. Canadian National #915 was scrapped as #80 in 1957, but seven members of the class managed to survive with at least one engine still operational.

The station was demolished in the 1960s but the town of Tottenham in co-operation with the Ontario Rail Foundation is preparing this very site for an operating steam railway. Two locomotives in paintings reproduced in this book . . . #136 and #1057 . . . are on the site, and may be operating within the year. Unfortunately, no Canadian National E-10 class Moguls are available to complete the scene.

## PARIS STATION, ONTARIO
## 1943

It's 10:30 a.m., arrival time at Paris Station for #17, Canadian National's famous "Inter-City Limited." It's 1943, the war is dragging into it's fourth year and trains throughout Canada are filled beyond capacity. New, more powerful locomotives are arriving on the system and one of the latest, a Northern Type 4-8-4, #6200, built by the Montreal Locomotive Works, heads #17 this morning. She rolls to a smooth stop, seems to be breathing a deep sigh, then waits the few minutes as baggage, mail, express and passengers are exchanged. In moments #6200 will ease on out of the station and upgrade toward Woodstock and London. By 8:20 p.m. the train will reach it's destination — Chicago, Illinois. #6200 will of course only run as far as Sarnia with this train due to International customs regulations, but another Northern (4-8-4) from the Systems Grand Trunk Western connection will wheel the "Limited" into Chicago.

The old brick station with it's orange tile roof and picturesque tower is gone now. Fortunately I photographed this little gem before it was demolished. Somehow, this station added a touch of class to the western Ontario town with its worldly name — Paris.

## ST. MARYS — "THE TOWN WORTH LIVING IN," ONTARIO
### 1957

Only two years from retirement, Mikado Type freight locomotive #3547 rolls a caboose hop across the high steel bridge not far from downtown St. Marys.

St. Marys, though not a large town, is similar to Paris and Port Hope in many pleasant ways. I sense a challenge in the beauty of their valleys, the old architecture and the railways, the necessary elements for a successful painting.

Canadian National Mikado #3547 was out of place here in Ontario. This locomotive along with 34 other sisters of the same class had spent their working years in the west since leaving the Montreal Locomotive Works in 1923. #3547 unlike the others had had bad luck and finally engine crews were relieved to see her sent to Stratford for major repairs in the mid 50s. It was hoped her luck would change if kept in the east so her final years were spent working out of Stratford. I think she made it home to Stratford this lovely September afternoon in 1957.

An interesting feature in the design and construction of Mikado #3547 and her 34 sister locomotives was the Belpaire boiler. This boiler is very easily identified by its squared-off shape as opposed to the cylindrical boilers found on most North American steam locomotives. Belpaire boilers were almost a standard feature in British and French steam locomotives. In my opinion, the Belpaire boiler makes this class of Canadian National locomotives more interesting and a challenge to paint.

## LONDON, ONTARIO, C.P.R. STATION 1955

Like most railroad stations of the steam era, London's Canadian Pacific station, built in the early 1900s, is located close to the centre of the city.

Here in the summer of 1955, the station is a place of activity. The engineer, having completed his inspection of #2806 according to the book, climbs back into the cab to await his signal to depart. Over on the north side of Richmond Street level crossing, a conductor and his brakeman stand chewing the fat while waiting for #2806 to pull out. Once #2806 has left, they can proceed with their work of switching cars on the siding to make up their freight train. They are possibly looking at #2806 for the last time, and probably recalling how for as long as either of them can remember Canadian Pacific's powerful Hudson #2806 and her sisters regularly hauled most of C.P.'s mainline name trains such as the "Canadian," the "Dominion" and the "Royal York." The conductor and the brakeman know that the steam age is coming to a close and they are probably wondering about the future of Hudson #2806 as well as their own futures.

Although London's C.P.R. station still stands, it is no longer a centre of activity. Not only have the steam trains gone that were once the centre of the city's vitality and transport, but even the modern diesel trains have been eclipsed by highway transport. London Station now stands desolate, bypassed by progress, with the future seemingly belonging to the suburbs.

## COUNTRY CROSSING, ONTARIO 1942

Take yourself back (if you're old enough), or just imagine it if you're not old enough. You're walking down this country road, past the clapboard or brick houses that have clustered into a small village near this crossing. There are no fast-food outlets nearby. No advertising billboards. Not too many cars, either. You hear a shrill whistle and look up to see a puff of steam as #1212 rolls into view, curving past the water tank, and crosses the road in front of you. You watch as #1212 slips into the distance, into the future.

Surrounded by the peace and security of this Ontario rural landscape of 1942, it might be difficult to realize that the world was locked in the deadly struggle of yet another global war. Young Canadians, who had grown up in this peaceful corner of the world, have left to cross oceans and confront the enemy. You might think back to the First World War, "the war to end all wars," and console yourself that *surely* this second global conflict would finish the job. You might look at the lad on the bike and think thankfully that he's too young to fight this war. He will enjoy the peace that *must* result from this second great effort to "end all wars." And #1212 will roll on forever, whistling its greeting to a secure country crossing.

Today the road is straight, multi-laned and possibly there's an overpass where the level crossing used to be ... or, maybe, there's no track at all. Certainly, there's no #1212. The old Ten Wheeler (4-6-0) was built in 1906 by the Montreal Locomotive Works for the Canadian Northern Railroad. It worked until 1950, a reliable, functional creation of a more secure epoch. It was scrapped in December of that year. The year the Korean War started. The boy on the bike is old enough to have participated in that conflict.

Superhighways, speeding cars, fast food outlets from chicken to fish fingers and umpteen varieties of hamburger. And square apartments and condos instead of clapboard and brick cottages. And forty major wars since 1942. No country crossing anywhere is secure from enemy missiles. And something besides #1212 is missing because of it all.

## GODERICH C.N. STATION, ONTARIO 1941

Goderich had two outstanding examples of Canadian railroad architecture. Not long ago on a trip to one of my favourite Ontario towns, I found both still stood and were in reasonably good condition.

Clean white snow surrounding the old Grand Trunk station presented me with an uncluttered backdrop which accented its romantic architectural character, turrets and all. The sight of this station in the winter instantly took me back to a similar setting when I was a boy and used to find the station the most exciting place in town.

It was always an adventure to be around the station at train time. Sometimes I was there to see my father off and it usually meant an opportunity to climb into the cab of Dad's engine. I'll bet that's where these two youngsters will end up before the conductor shouts "all aboard."

The scene is set in the winter of 1941. With the war into it's third year, gas was rationed. A few cars were around in winter but horses and sleighs were still in common use and shared the road with cars. Rail traffic was heavy and extra trains were quite a common occurence. Long distance travel was still train travel and service men were always on the move along with civilians. Though no service men are in sight, they could not be far away as a large air training school was in operation only a short distance north of Goderich. A farmer has just delivered cordwood by sleigh to keep the fires going in the station stoves.

The locomotive ready to leave for Stratford is one of Canadian National's numerous light Pacific Type passenger locomotives #5565. Passenger power of this type was used over the entire system and most notably throughout southwestern Ontario on branch line passenger train service until 1959. With the demise of steam power in 1959 most of the branchline passenger service was discontinued as well. Goderich lost its rail passenger service not long after.

Goderich CN station was built in 1911 to replace an old wooden structure which had served the Grand Trunk since the line opened in 1855.

## PORT McNICOLL, ONTARIO 1938

Although not a large village, Port McNicoll did have two stations. One was some distance from the village and in close proximity to the harbour which was a very busy place during the Great Lakes navigation season. The harbour featured a large grain elevator but also catered to passenger steamship traffic.

A popular Canadian vacation during the first half of the 20th century was a transcontinental journey which could include a Great Lakes cruise. One could leave Toronto by train for Port McNicoll, board one of the Canadian Pacific's two luxury cruise ships... the *Keewatin* or *Assiniboia*... to Port Arthur, then continue by train to the west coast.

Here, in the summer of 1938, the captain of the *Keewatin* prepares to dock his ship alongside Port McNicoll's harbour station just as the boat train arrives behind Canadian Pacific's light Pacific #2223 from Toronto. In a few minutes boat and train will exchange their passengers and steam off in opposite directions only to repeat the same scene a week later.

One of Canadian Pacific's many light passenger locomotives, #2223 was built by the Montreal Locomotive Works in February, 1911 and worked faithfully around southern Ontario until it was retired and scrapped in February, 1959.

## TEMAGAMI, ONTARIO
### 1937

Grandad cautions his grandson as they both cross Highway 11 near Temagami, Ontario to watch the spectacular passage of Temiskaming and Northern Ontario's train #46. Of great interest to the old man and the young boy is the new T. & N.O. locomotive. It is one of the four large and powerful Northern Types (4-8-4) built for the company by the Canadian Locomotive Works in Kingston.

In 1937, locomotive #1100 was less than a year old and it is quite possible that Grandad and Grandson have never witnessed its thundering passage before. During the relatively short time that the Northern Types served on the T. & N.O. they were subjected to a number of livery changes. The company's colour scheme shown here was undoubtedly the most sophisticated.

Technically and aesthetically, Northern Type locomotives of the Temiskaming and Northern Ontario railway were closely related to those built for Canadian National and Canadian Pacific, featuring the massive-looking European-type smoke deflectors.

I have painted this train speeding south toward North Bay where the T. & N.O. could connect with Toronto via C.N. and C.P. lines, but the main track of the T. & N.O. actually ran northward through Cochrane to Moosonee on James Bay with branches to Timmins and Noranda. Our vantage point is just south of the village of Temagami about 65 miles north of North Bay. Note that in 1937 Highway 11 was still just gravel ... and it remained that way until after World War II.

## COCHRANE UNION STATION, ONTARIO 1937

The station at Cochrane was designed and built by the Temiskaming and Northern Ontario Railway about 1909. Its architectural style was unique. The station survived two catastrophic forest fires which levelled the town, first in 1911 and again in 1916. A Union Station status developed about 1911 as the National Transcontinental, constructed by the Federal Government, pushed westward through Cochrane to Winnipeg from Quebec.

Today the station stands and is still used by the Ontario Northland and the Canadian National but its architectural richness was destroyed by a renovation and remodelling programme in the 1960s.

One warm Sunday evening during the summer of 1937, a Canadian National westbound freight lumbers slowly past the station. The Mountie in full uniform is not positioned there for casual tourist curiosity. These are still depression days and every freight leaving Cochrane, without exception, carried it's share of non-revenue passengers. Countless unemployed men moved from town to town looking for work. The Mounties had the unpleasant task of removing the unwanted passengers and redirecting them in an effort to reduce the possibility of large numbers collecting in one location.

To the right, on the T. & N.O. platform, activity centers on the arrival of locomotive #101 pulling train #47 from Toronto. In Cochrane, townsfolk met at the station to socialize, not just to meet trains. My feeling is that the lady with her Scottie is on a social visit, wanting a few words with the resplendent Mountie . . .

## THE BATHING BEACH, COCHRANE, ONTARIO
## 1940

This painting might be titled, "Fresh Air and Sunshine" or "A Great Town to Live In."

My home town, Cochrane, Ontario wasn't very large as towns go and it was a long way north in relation to Toronto and southern Ontario. Summers were short and winters were long, but this thriving little railroad town had a crystal-clear lake right in its centre. As kids, our daily activities were strongly influenced by Lake Commando. In summer, we swam and fished in it from the time the ice disappeared. In winter, we skated on it until the snow got too deep. Then we skied on and around it. Even our High School was built right on Lake Commando's shore.

In 1940, trains, cars and people all seemed to converge into a mosaic of activity at the south end of Lake Commando. This end of the lake was dominated by the railway's main line and yards, and by the swimming beach. We hardly took any notice of the odd whiff of smoke or steam from passing trains. The bathing beach was very pleasant ... backed by lush stands of birch and poplar trees. Later in the 40s, the city council decided the beach should be moved to the north side of Lake Commando, away from the trains.

Up near the station, a Canadian National Pacific locomotive #5281 eases onto it's train, #12, "The Quebecer." Within minutes, #5281 will head east with #12 train bound for Quebec and Montreal. Such happy memories!

## PRAIRIE LANDSCAPE, MANITOBA
### 1946

As the morning sun climbs into the late summer sky, a work-worn Canadian National, Mikado Type freight locomotive, #3552 sorts out loaded grain cars and spots fresh empties. Keep the grain moving to market without interruption in this, the busiest period of the year for the western wheat growers, and the railroads!

Down at the station, the westbound "Continental Limited" stops briefly, takes water, exchanges express mail, passengers and then steams west toward the Pacific.

Heavy concentration of minerals in Prairie water presented the railways with a serious problem. Used in the locomotive steam boilers, it had a devastating effect and increased the cost of maintenance alarmingly. Canadian National, in an attempt to solve this problem had locomotives designed and built, starting in 1923, specifically for western operation. Mikado #3552 was one of the first such locomotives built by the Montreal Locomotive Works to solve this problem.

In the late 1920s and early 30s, larger, heavier Mikado and Texas Type locomotives followed with improved water handling apparatus ... the 3800's and the 4300's respectively. The 3800 Mikado's and 4300 Texas Types are featured in two paintings in this book ... Rosebud, Alberta, and Winter in Saskatchewan.

## WINTER IN SASKATCHEWAN
## 1952

While caught in the grip of another sub-zero winter, this little Saskatchewan grain centre is rudely shaken from its early morning drowsiness by the shattering exhaust of a Canadian National eastbound freight. The locomotive, a heavy Mikado type (2-8-2) freight locomotive #3800, slows as the engineer prepares to pick up new orders on the fly from the operator on the platform. Ever mindful of the extreme cold, he wants to keep his tonnage rolling at a fair clip to avoid stalling in the cut not far east of this station. An event not appreciated in this climate by either the train crew or management is a stalled train which can take hours to restart.

Standing like great wooden sentinels, prairie elevators guard the rail sidings filled with grain cars. The ponderous Santa Fe Type (2-10-2), Class T-4-a, built in 1929, #4317 shown here to the right, has been sorting through car-filled sidings for contributions to its westbound extra. #4317 was one of 33 in her class and one of 93 Santa Fe Type locomotives used on the Canadian National until the end of steam in 1960. The 4300's were built to cope with western hard water problems as were the 3800, S-4 Mikado's.

Within an hour the only sound that will be heard over the frigid silence will be the sound of frost cracking in the wood sheathing on the grain elevators.

## ROSEBUD, ALBERTA
## 1948

One of Canadian National's "Mikado Type" (2-8-2) heavy freight locomotives, #3801, rolls eastbound tonnage past ranks of colourful grain elevators in Rosebud, Alberta. Rosebud, a little prairie grain centre, lies just a few miles northeast of Calgary in beautiful rolling Alberta wheatland.

But soon our eastbound freight will encounter the infamous "Badlands" around Drumheller where tortuous curves and grades will tax all 60,000 pounds of tractive effort that the 12 year old Kingston-built Mikado can produce. Like her sister locomotive #3800, depicted in the painting, "Winter in Saskatchewan," #3801 was designed to cope with the mineral-rich prairie water.

Only six S-4 class Mikado (2-8-2) Type locomotives were built for the Canadian National Railways and unfortunately none were saved from scrapping in 1957. In my opinion, they were the most aesthetically pleasing steam locomotives to ever run on the Canadian National. One of them would have made an outstanding exhibit at a transport museum.

## BANFF STATION, ALBERTA 1949

It is 1949 and Canadian Pacific still carries the greater proportion of tourists to and from Banff in the Canadian Rockies ... but the end of steam, the end of open observation cars, and the end of heavyweight passenger coaches bearing Canadian Pacific red is only five years away.

Usually trains like "The Mountaineer" and "The Dominion" were assigned newer, massive "Selkirk Type" locomotives to haul them over the spine of the Rockies from Calgary to Revelstoke. Occasionally, however, train scheduling and maintenance demands forced the substitution of smaller and less powerful G4 "Pacific Types" (4-6-2), like #2707 pictured here. There's no doubt that a double header of two "Pacific Types" would have been more realistic than just the one locomotive, but I have taken artistic licence in order to make #2707 the centre of the composition and to capture the character of a typical Canadian Pacific passenger train of the period.

The activity in this painting is typical of any busy day in mid-summer. The tours coming and going on special pullman cars are being loaded by porters from the Banff Springs Hotel. The hotel bus is backed up to the platform so it can exchange the mountains of luggage with dispatch, without delaying any train if possible. One train follows another so the action flows on ... Cooks Tours — Cartan Tours — Rocky Mountain Tours. The Mountaineer arrives and departs; "Dominions," two of them in each direction heading for Montreal, Toronto and Vancouver. If you were a porter, you might find time in an unexpected lull to grab a sandwich and a Coke before the next surge of vacationers landed on the platform.

## THE ROYAL TRAIN, ALBERTA 1939

In 1939, King George VI and Queen Elizabeth toured Canada from coast-to-coast in the longest and most elaborate royal visit ever made by a reigning monarch and his consort. Canadian Pacific and Canadian National Railways shared in the extensive transportation arrangements.

A Royal Train was assembled utilizing five cars each from the two railroads plus two vice-regal cars normally used by the Governor General of Canada. The twelve car train was specially finished in Royal Blue and Silver livery. Canadian Pacific supplied one locomotive, #2850 to handle the train over it's 3000 mile share of the tour. For the occasion, #2850, one of the Railroads new streamlined, H-1-d, Hudson Type passenger locomotives was equipped with a stainless steel boiler jacket and a paint scheme of royal blue, midnight blue and silver. Appropriate Royal crests appeared on the smokebox and tender. Royal Crowns of cast metal were mounted on the running board skirts, a later distinguishing feature of the 45 streamlined Hudsons, by Royal decree. The Royal Hudsons.

My painting picks up the Royal Train just after entering the Rockies on it's way to Banff after a late afternoon departure from Calgary, Alberta, late in May, 1939.

## "CONQUERING THE PASS," BRITISH COLUMBIA
## 1952

Unassisted, a massive "Selkirk Type" (2-10-4) muscles its eastbound Canadian Pacific express upgrade along the turbulent Kicking Horse River to its source — the crest of the infamous Kicking Horse Pass, the Great Divide.

A small group of hikers have stopped for a rest on the opposite bank of the river and are well positioned to watch the Selkirk's titanic struggle against grade and gravity. Within a year, though, this great struggle up the pass will resound with the deep growl of diesels and not with the thunder of steam.

The first twenty Selkirks were built in 1929 by the Montreal Locomotive Works and were unstreamlined, like #5902 shown here. In 1938, the Montreal Locomotive Works turned out ten more Selkirks which were semi-streamlined. The final six Selkirks, all semi-streamlined, were delivered in 1949.

The Selkirk Type was designed specifically to manage Canadian Pacific's brutal mainline through the Rocky Mountains and Selkirk Mountains. Although most Canadians do not distinguish between these two mountain ranges, calling all the western mountains "the Rockies," the Selkirk range is actually quite distinct. For one thing, it is much older than "the Rockies," and composed of generally harder rock. The Selkirk Range is characterized by hard, unforgiving triangular peaks that are very steep, presenting a much greater challenge than the Rockies. The Selkirk locomotives, designed to defeat the mountain barriers of the west, were named in honour of their toughest opponent. Technically, the Selkirks were the Canadian version of the American "Texas Type" (2-10-4) locomotive.

## LAKE SHUSWAP, BRITISH COLUMBIA
## 1937

One of the fondest memories of my first trip by rail across Canada in July, 1949, relates to the evening our Canadian Pacific train, "The Dominion", rolled along the south shore of Lake Shuswap in mid-British Columbia. The rails hug the shoreline for many miles along this beautiful expanse of lake from Sicamous to Salmon Arm. The line fights to maintain its grip on the rocky, mountain terrain and in this way has a close relationship with the lake.

After nearly forty years, I decided (as with many other of my paintings) to step back in time ... to try to record this magnificent landscape and my first impressions of that warm summer evening. First, I had to remove myself from the train in order to include it in the composition. Then by stepping back another ten years, to 1937, I could replace the trains Royal Hudson with one of Canadian Pacific's earlier passenger locomotives, a Pacific Type, #2709 in typical late 1930s C.P. livery. Here #2709, one of 18 locomotives in her class, all operating in Alberta and British Columbia, comes rolling into view.

Lake Shuswap, though not as accessible in the late 30s and 40s as it is to-day, was a popular fisherman's paradise. As we rolled along, fishermen who had landed large catches would scramble to display their good fortune to delighted train passengers.

## THE ROYAL HUDSON, BRITISH COLUMBIA
## 1986

The largest steam locomotive to operate in regular service on the North American continent went into service on June 20th, 1974.

Royal Hudson #2860, originally built for the Canadian Pacific Railway by the Montreal Locomotive Works in 1940, became an instant success as British Columbia Railway's feature locomotive.

New, regularly scheduled, daily runs each summer since 1974 have been heavily booked in advance. Many claim the 6 hour excursions to Squamish and return are too short to recapture the flavour and nostalgia of the great days of steam.

West Vancouver municipal council ammended their noise by-law to permit the blowing of the Royal Hudson's distinctive whistle heralding each trip through the community and over this bridge at Capilano creek.

The forty-first member of Canadian Pacific's great fleet of forty-six Royal Hudsons and the first Royal Hudson to be built complete with the attractive Royal Crowns mounted to her running boards, #2860 spent all her years of service heading the railway's famous Transcontinental "The Dominion" between Vancouver and Revelstoke. By the mid-1950s, replacement power in the form of the diesel took over. Fortunately, someone had the foresight to realize the potential left in such a beautiful machine. Hence the great success of the steam excursions to Squamish and return.

# YOHO, BRITISH COLUMBIA 1932

Yoho in the Cree language means "how wonderful!", and it is an apt description of this location because everyone who views the valley and the surrounding peaks, except railroad men, say exactly that.

Canadian Pacific's Yoho Station accommodates an operator and not much else, and for good reason. Yoho Station is sited in one of the worst locations for avalanches on C.P.'s mainline through the Canadian Rockies. Snow conditions on the "Big Hill" at Yoho are of prime concern to the crews of steam trains. The thunder of the locomotives could touch off an avalanche of snow that could sweep an entire train from the track.

This scene captures one of Canadian Pacific's big, burly "Mikado Type" (2-8-2) freight locomotives #5362 pulling upgrade from the water tank. A brief exchange occurs between the engine crew and the resident Yoho operator before the train tackles the long struggle of the "Big Hill."

Until the completion of the Trans Canada Highway through the Kicking Horse Pass in the late 1950s, a strategically located tea room and observation verandah very close to this station made it possible to watch trains on the Big Hill. You could see the trains as they entered the lower tunnel, snaked along past Yoho station up to the upper tunnel, and finally conquered the Big Hill and disappeared toward Lake Louise and Banff. The new highway in utilizing the original railway grade, forced the demolition of the old tea room, so now to enjoy the view, you have to get out of your car and stand by the side of the road.

## "SELKIRKS" ON THE "BIG HILL," BRITISH COLUMBIA
### 1951

Two giant "Selkirks", #5900 and #5921 demonstrate the true spectacle of steam under harness in the high drama of their assault on the Canadian Rockies' legendary Kicking Horse Pass. Their task here is to safely power Canadian Pacific's famous Transcontinental Express, "The Dominion" up the tortuous "Big Hill," over the Continental Divide to the mountain resorts of Lake Louise and Banff and on to the east. No small task. "The Big Hill" as it is known, presents these "Selkirks" with over 20 miles of 2.2% grade, grinding 12% curves and two suffocating spiral tunnels, enough to hold even the tandem effort of these two brutes to a mere 20 miles per hour on the eastbound journey. Characteristic of this rugged terrain are the heavy timber snowsheds located at critical points along the line. Their function, winter and summer, was to protect roadbed and rolling stock from devastating rock slides and avalanches. Regardless of their design, location and ruggedness, these snowsheds have proven no match for the massive slides which occur on occasion due to excessive snow, rock and water buildup. At least twice within the past forty years massive slides have struck this very location. Rail and telephone lines and the highway disappeared. More than a week of intensive digging and reworking was necessary to restore east-west communications. In the event of a great slide, approaching trains were warned by a complex signal system and were able to stop before any damage was done.

The setting chosen depicts #5900 built in 1929 and #5921, a later sister of 1938 vintage, hard at work on a late mid-summer afternoon in 1951, apparently unaware that by 1956 the last proud "Selkirk" would be gone, scrapped.

## "HILLCREST NUMBER 10," VANCOUVER ISLAND, BRITISH COLUMBIA
### 1950

High on a valley-spanning trestle in the heart of Vancouver Island, Hillcrest Lumber's "Climax Type" locomotive #10 struggles upgrade with a heavy drag of giant Douglas Fir and West Coast Cedar logs. Miles ahead, at tidewater, the wooden giants will meet their fate and be reduced to manageable and standardized proportions by busy saws. As building material, the timber will be shipped all over the world.

Steam traction continued in use on many logging operations until the 1960s when rail lines were replaced by roads, and when enormous trucks replaced the logging locomotives. Most of these interesting and unusual logging locomotives were scrapped, but Hillcrest #10 was saved to become a museum attraction in a dynamic exhibition. It now operates over a short section of logging rails a few miles from Victoria. Tourists watching Hillcrest #10 working can see how logs were moved in the days of steam.

Although such scenes are very picturesque and illustrate the sense of industry and commerce which were so admired in the early years of the century, it should be noted that the little locomotives certainly did their share in helping to wipe out the great stands of huge Douglas Fir and Spruce which once stood so proudly on the Island. Recently, the Government turned a smaller island near by into a National Park and in this way preserved some of the past.

107

# GLOSSARY OF RAILROAD TERMS

**BAD ORDER TRACK**
A rail siding set aside for the storage of cars needing repair.

**BALLOON STACK**
A wide, flaring locomotive smoke stack designed to prevent sparks from escaping. Balloon stacks were used mainly in lumber and logging operations.

**BIG HOOK**
A railroad crane used to salvage cars and locomotives which have been derailed due to accident or collision.

**BLEED**
The operation of removing air from brake lines of railroad equipment.

**BLOCK SIGNALS**
An arrangement of colour-coded lights, or semaphore signals, positioned at regular intervals along a railroad mainline to control the sequence of passing trains safely.

**BRAKEMAN**
A member of a freight or passenger train crew whose duties are to assist the Conductor in any way necessary in the operation of the train.

**BUMP**
Railroad slang for the exercise of seniority by firing, or replacing, a man.

**CAB**
The section of a locomotive where the controls are located, and which is designed to offer weather protection for the engineer and fireman.

**CABOOSE (CRUMMY, VAN, HACK)**
A special car attached to the rear of all freight trains to accommodate the train crew. The caboose is not usually shared with the engine crew. Most caboose designs incorporate some sort of viewing cupola, either on top or on the side, so that the length of the entire train can be casually inspected by the crew while the train is in motion.

**CABOOSE HOP**
A train consisting only of a locomotive and caboose.

**CALL BOY**
A boy or man whose duty is to summon train crews.

**CAMELBACK**
A locomotive with the cab astride the boiler instead of behind it. Also called a Mother Hubbard.

**CAR KNOCKER**
An inspector of railway rolling stock, or cars, so called because he must tap the wheels of cars to test for soundness.

**CENTRAL TRAFFIC CONTROL (C.T.C.)**
The modern system of controlling train traffic from a central location by the electrical activation of block signals on the tracks. Formerly, operators stationed along the line were informed by telegraph or telephone to change block signals manually. Now, one man at C.T.C. replaces many on-line operators.

CLERESTORY
A roofline design used on most pre-1930s passenger cars featuring a two-tier profile with ventilators placed along the raised central spine of the roof. This design has been superseded in modern times by a one-level flat roof with the necessary ventilators placed elsewhere.

CONDUCTOR
The senior and supervising member of a freight and passenger train crew.

CONNECTING RODS
Steel rods which couple drive wheels of a locomotive, or which activate valves, or which connect the piston with the primary drive wheel.

COUPLER
A mechanical device designed to connect railway cars and locomotives together which is activated by the impact of one car bumping gently into another car.

D-RAIL
A device attached to railway track, usually sidings, to prevent the passage of railway cars. It is generally used to keep rolling stock on sidings from accidentally moving onto mainlines. It may also be used to protect men working on a section of railway track.

DEAD HEAD
An empty car. A passenger riding on a free pass. A locomotive in need of repair and inoperative that is coupled into a train for transport to a repair facility.

DECK
Called the footplate in Britain, it is the floor of the cab on which the engineer and the fireman stand to perform most of their duties.

DIAMOND
The intersection of two railway tracks which are on the same level but meet at less than 90 degrees.

DINKY
A small, undersized locomotive.

DISTANT SIGNAL
A warning signal used to "pre-indicate" the significance of another signal not far ahead.

DIVISION
That section of a railroad track, or system of tracks, managed by a superintendent.

DOUBLE HEADER
A train pulled by two locomotives.

DRIVERS
The large wheels of a locomotive that are driven by a connecting rod from the piston. Sets of driving wheels are themselves coupled together by connecting rods, all deriving power from the piston.

ECCENTRIC ROD
A steel rod that is connected "off-center" on a wheel of revolving disc so that its motion is the "opposite" of the motion of the piston's connecting rod. Eccentric rods activate the valves on a steam engine.

EXTRA
A special train, or one not listed on prepared schedules.

FILL
Earth used to make a level road bed across a valley.

FISH PLATE
The flat plate that joins the butt ends of two rails together. It is attached to the sides of both rails by rivets.

FLAG
To protect the rear of a stopped train by having a brakeman walk to the back of the train with a conspicuous flag and stand there ready to wave a warning to any oncoming train. To have anyone not on the crew stop a train by waving arms, a flag or a lantern.

FROG
The portion of a switch which is grooved to accommodate the flange of railway wheels, so called because of its resemblance to the shape of a frog.

GAUGE
The distance between the two rails of a track.

GOAT
A small diesel or steam locomotive used only for shifting rolling stock in a rail yard.

HIGHBALL
To operate a train at excessive speed. An old railroading signal to "proceed ahead," so called from outmoded ball signals that were raised to indicate a clear track.

## HIGH IRON
The mainline railway track where traffic is strictly regulated by schedule or special orders.

## HOGGER
The engineer.

## HOOP
A large-diameter light-weight wooden hoop used by operators at stations to pass new orders to train crews without stopping the train.

## HOSTLER
A railway worker who maintains locomotives at a terminal or "roundhouse."

## HOT BOX
A wheel bearing that has run dry of oil and is red hot because of friction. If undetected it can set a car on fire or wreck a train if the wheel will not turn.

## IN THE CLEAR
A phrase denoting safe intervals between oncoming trains using the mainline.

## JOHNSON BAR
A long and stout hand-lever used to reverse locomotive valve gears in order to make a steam engine operate "in reverse." Depending on the size and power of a locomotive, operating the Johnson Bar could be a brutal job and could totally exhaust an engineer after an 8-hour shift. Eventually, air pressure systems were introduced to reverse the valve gears.

## LEAD TRACK
Trackage connecting a yard with the mainline.

## MARKER LAMPS (MARKERS)
Colour-coded lights, lanterns or flags that are displayed (2 in front, 2 in the rear) by mainline trains to indicate their status, "scheduled" or "extra;" or colour-coded lights, lanterns or flags on a train to warn of a following but disconnected section; or such signals to indicate the end of a train.

## ON-THE-FLY
Any operation undertaken while the train is in motion at normal speed.

## PILOT
A sturdy metal framework extending out in front of a locomotive and shaped to deflect any debris which might obstruct a track, and which is positioned sufficiently low to the track so that no object can pass beneath the wheels. "Pilot" is the British term for this device to prevent possible derailment, but it is commonly called a "cow-catcher" in North America.

## PILOT BEAM
Main support for the pilot, or "cow-catcher."

## POPS
Steam safety valve on a locomotive that is adjusted to maintain the steam pressure within safe limits.

## PULL THE PIN
To uncouple cars or a locomotive from a train.

## RED BOARD
A block signal displaying a red light or displaying a semaphore in the "STOP" position.

## REEFER
A refrigerator car.

## RIGHT-OF-WAY
The land on which railway track is laid, plus the required margin to either side.

## RIP RAP
Large stones used to prevent washouts of gravel rail road beds, usually employed on river banks or sea shore.

## RULE G
Railroad rule against drinking on duty.

## SAND DOME
Round-topped cylinder located on top of a locomotive boiler and filled with sand. The engineer can spill sand from this container onto the track ahead of the drivers to increase traction.

## SEAT BOX
The engineer's seat, or the fireman's seat, in a locomotive cab designed for the storage of personal articles.

## SECTION HAND
A track worker.

## SEMAPHORE
A type of signalling device that uses a moving arm that can be positioned for maximum visibility. The position of the arm itself may be a signal, or the arm may carry colour-coded lights or paint to convey meaning.

SHUNT
To shift railway rolling stock, usually in a yard or loading zone, for any purpose.

SLOW ORDER
A railway directive affecting a section where track is being repaired, where bridges are being repaired, or where climatic conditions have caused a deterioration of the road bed and reduced speed is necessary for safety.

SMOKE DEFLECTORS
A sheet metal cowling mounted on the front of a locomotive shaped to deflect air upwards at normal operating speed. The purpose is to deflect smoke and steam upward and clear of the cab and train.

SPOTTING
Placing cars where they can be loaded.

STEAM DOME
Round-topped cylinder located on top of a locomotive boiler which covers the mechanical valves that control the flow of steam to the pistons.

STOKER
Originally a worker who shoveled coal into a locomotive's fire-box, but later a mechanical conveyor that performed the same job.

TEA KETTLE
Any old locomotive, particularly a leaky one, or a small locomotive used on some narrow-gauge railways (also called a "Tea Pot").

TELL-TALES
An arrangement of hanging ropes placed above tracks that warn crewmen on car roofs that the train is approaching a low bridge or a tunnel.

TENDER
An independent but necessary component of a steam locomotive that is carried on its own wheels and holds fuel (coal or oil) and water.

THROAT
Entry track to a yard or terminal.

TORPEDO
A small explosive device that can be clamped to track and is activated by the front wheels of a moving locomotive. It is a signal device intended primarily to protect a stalled train on the track ahead in conditions of poor visibility.

TRACTIVE EFFORT
The measure of a steam locomotive's power. The force a locomotive can exert *in pounds* under controlled conditions. For example, a "Selkirk Type" locomotive could produce 77,200 pounds of pulling power.

TRAINMASTER
A railway employee who co-ordinates the work of the yardmaster and the roundhouse foreman. He reports directly to the superintendent.

TRESTLE
A wooden bridge structure capable of supporting a railway track.

WASH-OUT
Track ballast (the gravel bed of a railway track) washed away by water action.

WIG-WAG
A pendulum or arm which can be activated at rail crossings, containing flashing red lights or reflectors, to warn of an oncoming train.

WILDCAT
A runaway locomotive that has gone out of control and cannot be stopped by the engineer on board.

WYE
A configuration of track with three sections, and three switches, that enables a train to be turned in order to change direction.

YARDMASTER
A railway employee in charge of yard operations.

## INDEX OF COLOUR PLATES

9  THE NEWFIE BULLET, NEWFOUNDLAND, 1938

11  ST. MARGARET'S BAY, NOVA SCOTIA, 1944

13  AUTO CAMP GROUND, NOVA SCOTIA, 1925

15  THE WATER STOP, NEW BRUNSWICK, 1935

17  NUMBER 136 IN NEW BRUNSWICK, 1952

19  PRINCE EDWARD ISLAND, 1930

21  WINDSOR STATION, MONTREAL, QUEBEC, 1939

23  "DAILY EVENT," QUEBEC, 1934

25  LAURENTIAN SKI TRAIN, QUEBEC, 1944

27  "SO WHO NEEDS A RAILWAY?" ... PICTON, ONTARIO, 1925

29  OTTAWA UNION STATION, ONTARIO, 1953

31  MUSKOKA WHARF, ONTARIO, 1934

33  ALGONQUIN PARK STATION, ONTARIO, 1935

35  "GONE FISHING," ONTARIO, 1936

37  "CHARLIE'S WORLD," ONTARIO, 1946

39  THE DON STATION, TORONTO, ONTARIO, 1949

41  THE RAILROAD CHILDREN, TORONTO, ONTARIO, 1928

43  NORTH TORONTO STATION, ONTARIO, 1925

45  BATHURST STREET, TORONTO, ONTARIO, 1942

47  "THE INTERNATIONAL" STEAM SPECTACULAR, TORONTO, ONTARIO, 1931

49  SUNNYSIDE STATION, TORONTO, ONTARIO, 1935

51  WEST TORONTO STATION, ONTARIO, 1930

53  "SIR HENRY'S TIME MACHINE," WHITBY, ONTARIO, 1931

55  "HOME FOR CHRISTMAS," ONTARIO, 1937

57  SEPTEMBER AFTERNOON, ONTARIO, 1948

59  THE WINTER OF 1947, ONTARIO

61  TORONTO, HAMILTON & BUFFALO STATION, HAMILTON, ONTARIO, 1939

63  INGLEWOOD, ONTARIO, 1939

65  WINTER NIGHT, INGLEWOOD, ONTARIO, 1948

67  TOTTENHAM, ONTARIO, 1931

69  PARIS STATION, ONTARIO, 1943

71  ST. MARYS — "THE TOWN WORTH LIVING IN," ONTARIO, 1957

73  LONDON, ONTARIO, C.P.R. STATION, 1955

75  COUNTRY CROSSING, ONTARIO, 1942

77  GODERICH C.N. STATION, ONTARIO, 1941

79  PORT McNICOLL, ONTARIO, 1938

81  TEMAGAMI, ONTARIO, 1937

83  COCHRANE UNION STATION, ONTARIO, 1937

85  THE BATHING BEACH, COCHRANE, ONTARIO, 1940

87  PRAIRIE LANDSCAPE, MANITOBA, 1946

89  WINTER IN SASKATCHEWAN, 1952

91  ROSEBUD, ALBERTA, 1948

93  BANFF STATION, ALBERTA, 1949

95  THE ROYAL TRAIN, ALBERTA, 1939

97  "CONQUERING THE PASS," BRITISH COLUMBIA, 1952

99  LAKE SHUSWAP, BRITISH COLUMBIA, 1937

101  THE ROYAL HUDSON, BRITISH COLUMBIA, 1986

103  YOHO, BRITISH COLUMBIA, 1932

105  "SELKIRKS" ON THE "BIG HILL," BRITISH COLUMBIA, 1951

107  "HILLCREST NUMBER 10," VANCOUVER ISLAND, BRITISH COLUMBIA, 1950